972.91 DOW

Che GUEVARA

DAVID DOWNING

Heinemann

£8.75

www.heinemann.co.uk/library
Visit our website to find out more information about Heinemann Library books.

To order:
☎ Phone 44 (0) 1865 888066
🖹 Send a fax to 44 (0) 1865 314091
💻 Visit the Heinemann Bookshop at www.heinemann.co.uk/library to browse our catalogue and order online.

First published in Great Britain by Heinemann Library, Halley Court, Jordan Hill, Oxford OX2 8EJ, part of Harcourt Education Ltd.

Heinemann is a registered trademark of Harcourt Education Ltd.

Produced for Heinemann by Discovery Books Ltd

Editorial: Patience Coster, Nicole Irving, Andrew Solway and Jennifer Tubbs
Design: Ian Winton
Illustrator: Stefan Chabluk
Picture research: Rachel Tisdale
Production: Séverine Ribierre

Originated by Dot Gradations
Printed and bound in China by South China Printing Company

ISBN 0 431 13879 6 (hardback)
07 06 05 04 03
10 9 8 7 6 5 4 3 2 1

ISBN 0 431 13887 7 (paperback)
08 07 06 05 04
10 9 8 7 6 5 4 3 2 1

British Library Cataloguing in Publication Data
Downing, David
  Che Guevara. – (Leading lives)
  980'.033'092

A full catalogue record for this book is available from the British Library.

Acknowledgements
The publishers would like to thank the following for permission to reproduce photographs: Bettman/Corbis: pp. **22**, **30**, **33**, **36**; Camera Press: pp. **6**, **9**, **11**; Corbis: pp. **15** (Jim Zuckerman), **39**, **40**, **42**; Hulton Archive: pp. **18**, **27**, **29**; Perfecto Romero/CSC: p. **44**; Peter Newark's American Pictures: pp. **24**, **25**; Popperfoto: pp. **4**, **21**, **23**, **26**, **32**, **48**, **51**; Popperfoto/Reuters: p. **54**; Rex Features: pp. **5**, **17**, **35**; South American Pictures: p. **52** (Rolando Pujol).

Cover photograph of Che Guevara reproduced with permission of Popperfoto.

Every effort has been made to contact copyright holders of any material reproduced in this book. Any omissions will be rectified in subsequent printings if notice is given to the publishers.

8·75   **Contents**   A08408

1 Life after death   4

2 Childhood and youth   6

3 Motorcycle odyssey   12

4 Guatemala and Fidel   18

5 Comandante!   24

6 Falling out with the USA   30

7 Falling out with the Soviets   38

8 Failure in Africa   44

9 Death in Bolivia   48

10 Legacy   52

Timeline   56

Key people of Che Guevara's time   58

Places to visit and further reading   60

Glossary   61

Index   64

Any words appearing in the text in bold, **like this**, are explained in the Glossary.

1 Life after death

In July 1997, in the middle of the South American winter, a small group of Cubans arrived in the Bolivian town of Vallegrande to begin the hunt for the body of their national hero. The Argentine-born Ernesto 'Che' Guevara had fought in the Cuban **revolutionary** war some forty years earlier, and been a leading figure in the government which emerged from the revolutionaries' victory. In 1967 he had perished in an attempt to kick-start a new **revolution** in Bolivia, and until recently it had been believed that his murderers had **cremated** his body. Now new evidence suggested that he had been buried near Vallegrande's small airfield. After several weeks of searching, the bodies of three men were unearthed, and one of them was identified as Che's.

Che's body was flown north to Cuba, where he had made his name as a **guerrilla** fighter and political leader. Cuba had launched him on his short but dazzling career as a revolutionary hero, and turned him into something almost

unique – a world-famous enemy of both the USA and the Soviet Union, of both international **capitalism** and established international **communism**.

◀ Che Guevara's remains leave the Cuban capital, Havana, for burial on 14 October 1997. In the background a government building is adorned with the Cuban flag and an image of Guevara's face.

While most people praised one system and criticized the other, Che had seemed keenly aware of the flaws in both. Now Cuba welcomed him back. More than thirty years after his death, hundreds of thousands of people queued to pay their respects to the body of the man in the flag-draped casket.

Che Guevara is not only remembered in Cuba. In cities, towns and villages throughout **Latin America** images of his face are stencilled on the walls of buildings, a continuing inspiration for all those who seek **radical** change and social justice. In the richer parts of the world, countries in Europe and North America for example, the same face stares out from T-shirts, posters, books and CD cases. In these countries Che's face has become an image of youthful protest, of saying 'no' to the way the world is run. But his face has become so familiar that at times it has come to seem like a mere fashion accessory, a badge of cool worn by people who have little idea what he stood for.

▲ A multi-coloured Che Guevara in Havana in 1993. Thirty years after his death, Guevara's image is still widely associated with revolution and social justice.

So who was Ernesto 'Che' Guevara, and why is his memory still so precious to so many? How did an Argentinian with a serious life-long illness come to be fighting in a Cuban revolutionary war? How was it possible, at the height of the **Cold War** between the USA and the Soviet Union, for him to fall out with both them? And what, in the end, led him from Cuba to that grave beside the airfield in the small Bolivian town of Vallegrande?

Childhood and youth

Ernesto Guevara de la Serna, the future Che Guevara, was born on 14 May 1928 in the Argentine city of Rosario. He was the first child of Ernesto Guevara Lynch and Celia de la Serna y Llosa. During the next fifteen years his parents would have four more children: Celia, Ana María, Roberto and Juan Martín.

Ernesto Sr, whose family roots in Argentina stretched back many generations, could consider himself a member of the country's **nobility**. His wife Celia had inherited much money and property. Despite this wealth, the family was known for its **socialist** opinions and its desire for a fairer society. Like Celia,

Ernesto Sr's mother Ana Lynch – the only grandmother that young Ernesto ever knew – was an active campaigner for women's rights. Celia's sister, Carmen, and her poet husband, Cayetano, were both members of the Argentine **Communist** Party.

A lifelong affliction

During the first years of young Ernesto's life the family lived in San Isidro, close to the Argentine capital Buenos Aires.

◀ *Ernesto Guevara de la Serna as a small boy in San Isidro, Argentina.*

Asthma

Asthma is an illness characterized by a difficulty in breathing. It is caused by excessive tightening of the muscles of the tubes connecting the throat with the lungs. The muscles make the tubes narrower, so that it is hard for air to pass through them. In serious asthma attacks it becomes almost impossible for the person to breathe, which means that his or her life may be in danger. Infections, physical activity and allergies can all increase the frequency and add to the severity of attacks. Asthma can be treated with drugs, which lessen the symptoms.

It was here, a few days before his second birthday, that Ernesto had his first **asthma** attack. For three terrifying years these attacks continued on a more or less daily basis. Slowly but surely, medical care, parental devotion and the boy's own efforts combined to make the illness more manageable, but the rest of Ernesto's life would be coloured by his continuing struggles with asthma.

The early years of scares and alarms created a lifelong bond between mother and son. Through the many bed-ridden days, Celia would read and talk to Ernesto, encouraging a sense of curiosity about the world and stimulating his love of learning.

The young Ernesto would have a balloon of oxygen on hand to help him through his asthma attacks. However, according to his father, he would only use it at the last minute. 'He did not want to depend on this treatment, and he tried to bear the attack as long as he could, but when he could no longer stand it and his face was turning purple from the choking, he would wriggle and point to his mouth to indicate that it was time. The oxygen relieved him immediately.'

'El Loco'

Around 1935, the family moved to the hill town of Alta Gracia, where the cleaner air was thought to be good for Ernesto's illness. Here he started attending school, only occasionally at first, but with increasing regularity between the ages of ten and eleven. When he was too ill to go to school, he studied at home, determined to make up for what he was missing.

Encouraged by his father, he showed a similarly resolute attitude to sports and other physical activities. He was always eager to prove that his illness would not hold him back or limit him in any way, and as a teenager he acquired the nickname 'El Loco' (the mad one) for his recklessness. He jumped off high rocks into rivers, tightrope-walked his way across deep ravines, and rode his bike along railway tracks.

Despite his physical weakness, Ernesto was clearly a natural leader from an early age. One fellow pupil later told how 'the children followed him around a lot in the schoolyard; he would climb up a big tree that was there, and all the kids stood around him as if he were the leader, and when he ran the others followed behind him; it was clear that he was the boss.'

Growing up

In 1936, when Ernesto was eight years old, the **Spanish Civil War** broke out in Europe. Most Argentinians had Spanish roots, and the conflict was followed with great interest throughout the country. This was particularly true of the Guevara household in Alta Gracia. Ernesto's Uncle Cayetano went to Spain as a newspaper correspondent, and his family came to live with the Guevaras. This meant that the young Ernesto was able to follow the progress of the war very closely. He hung a huge map of Spain on his bedroom wall and tried to create a small-scale battlefield in the back garden.

▲ *The 17-year-old Ernesto with his family in Mar del Plata in 1945. From left to right: Ernesto, his mother Celia, sister Celia, brothers Roberto and Juan Martín, father Ernesto and sister Ana Maria.*

In 1943 the family moved some 40 kilometres to the much larger city of Córdoba, where Ernesto was already attending high school (for the past year he had been travelling to and fro each day on the bus). He was only an average student, doing well in those subjects that interested him, like literature and **philosophy**, and not so well in those that did not, like music and physics. He swam, played tennis and golf, and grew to love chess. At this point in his life he particularly enjoyed the challenge of playing rugby. If, as often happened, he suffered an asthma attack mid-game, he would leave the field to give himself an injection of **adrenalin**.

Student

In 1946 Ernesto finished high school and took a part-time job with the local roads department. His family were in the process of moving to Buenos Aires, but the eighteen-year-old Ernesto seemed determined to stay in Córdoba to study engineering at the local university. He may have wanted to stay near his friends, or he may have been eager to leave the family home, which in recent years had become the scene of many bitter fights between his parents over money and his father's affairs with other women.

In Buenos Aires, Ernesto's grandmother became seriously ill, and Celia needed her son's help in caring for the old woman during her final months. Celia had herself recently undergone surgery for breast cancer, and it seems likely that the combination of medical events – his mother's illness, his grandmother's death, and his own long struggle with asthma – persuaded Ernesto to study medicine instead of engineering. In 1947 he registered at the Faculty of Medicine in Buenos Aires, and spent the next four years as a medical student, specializing in the treatment of **allergies**.

His life became that of a hard-working, hard-playing student. He never took any care of his appearance – his hair was always uncombed, his shoelaces untied – and his rare baths earned him a new nickname: 'El Chancho' (the pig). None of this seemed to affect his popularity with the girls. By 1950 he was involved with a girl named Chichina, whom he had met several years earlier in Córdoba.

His love for Chichina, however, was more than matched by his love of travel. During one summer vacation, he toured northern Argentina on a motorized bicycle, visiting his old

Córdoba friend Alberto Granado at the **leper colony** where he worked. In another vacation he worked as a deckhand on a merchant ship, visiting Brazil, Trinidad, Venezuela and the southern ports of Argentina. Late in 1951, Alberto told Ernesto that he had taken a job in another leper colony in far-off Venezuela, and suggested that the two of them travel there together by motorbike. Ernesto said yes. His desire to see the world was stronger than either his love for Chichina or his commitment to his medical studies.

▼ *Ernesto on the motorized bicycle he used for travelling around Argentina in his student days.*

Motorcycle odyssey

Ernesto and Alberto set off on their voyage to Venezuela in mid-January 1952, at the height of the South American summer. But they soon ran into difficulties. Alberto's Norton 500cc motorcycle, which he called *La Poderosa* (the powerful one) broke down with alarming frequency on the unpaved roads. The two men were thrown off with distressing regularity – nine times on one particularly bad day. Off the road, they added to their own problems by carelessly climbing a mountain and leaving it too late to get down before nightfall.

One night, knowing that a puma was prowling in the area, a panicky Ernesto fired the two men's revolver in the direction of the two eyes glowing in the darkness, only to discover that he had shot the dog of the farmer with whom they were staying. Things went from bad to worse when, a few days later, he picked up a forwarded letter from Chichina saying that their relationship was over.

Ernesto and Alberto's adventures continued in

Che's travels 1951–6
→ Dec 1951–Aug 1952
→ Aug 1953–Dec 1953
--→ The voyage of the *Granma*

▲ A map showing Ernesto's travels through South and Central America between the years of 1951 and 1956.

Latin America

Latin America is the name usually given to those parts of the Americas which were conquered by Spain and Portugal in the 15th and 16th centuries, and which remain Spanish and Portuguese speaking. It includes all of Central America and Mexico, the Spanish-speaking islands of the Caribbean, and almost all of continental South America. The populations include the descendants of those **indigenous** Indians conquered by the European **colonial** powers, the descendants of slaves brought from Africa, European **immigrants**, and various combinations of the above resulting from inter-marriage.

Traditionally, Europe and North America used Latin America as a source of raw materials – minerals and food products. In each country, small groups who controlled the production of these raw materials – the local elites – grew rich, but the mass of the population remained very poor. By the time of Ernesto Guevara's birth, almost all Latin American countries were politically independent of their former colonial masters, but their economies were still largely controlled by North American and European businesses working in combination with rich and powerful local people. The vast majority of the ordinary people remained caught up in lifelong struggles to feed, clothe and house themselves.

Chile. *La Poderosa* was slowly falling to pieces, and it finally collapsed altogether on one steep, Chilean hill. They managed to persuade a lorry driver to give them a ride to the Chilean capital, Santiago, but *La Poderosa* was beyond repair. For the rest of their journey the two travellers had to depend on lifts from others.

The shadow of injustice

In the Chilean port of Valparaíso, Ernesto agreed to visit a friend of the bar-owner with whom they were staying, an old and poverty-stricken woman with **asthma**. He was horrified to see the conditions in which she was living. 'The poor thing was in an awful state,' he wrote. 'It is in cases like this, when a doctor knows he is powerless… that he longs for change, a change which would prevent the injustice of a system in which, until a month ago, this poor old woman had had to earn her living as a waitress, wheezing and panting.'

Heading north

In Valparaíso, Ernesto and Alberto smuggled themselves on board a ship heading north, emerging from hiding only when the ship was at sea. Disembarking in northern Chile, they crossed the desert to visit the vast copper mine at Chuquicamata, and then journeyed north into Peru. For the next two months they travelled through the mountains, often sharing the backs of lorries with groups of **Andean Indians**. These people and their cultures fascinated Ernesto. He was also enormously impressed by the remains of the **Inca** civilization that he and Alberto saw in Peru on the shores of Lake Titicaca, in the old Inca capital Cuzco, and in the long-lost Inca city of Machu Picchu.

FOR A MAP OF GUEVARA'S TRAVELS, SEE PAGE 12.

The two men were often cold in the mountains, and frequently hungry. In order to get food they would perform their 'anniversary routine', casually telling strangers that it was exactly a year ago that they set out on their trip. How sad, they would add, that they didn't have the money to celebrate. The strangers would buy them a drink, which they would happily accept. Ernesto, however, would reluctantly refuse a second drink. When asked to explain why, he would say that in

▲ *The ruined Inca city of Machu Picchu, which Guevara visited on both his journeys through South America.*

Argentina it was the custom to eat and drink at the same time. The strangers would then buy them food. According to Ernesto, their trick to win a free meal never failed.

Amazonia

From the Peruvian capital Lima, Ernesto and Alberto headed back across the Andes and down into the upper reaches of the **Amazon basin**. Ernesto had suffered many asthma attacks in the thin air of the mountains, but down in the tropical lowlands they grew more frequent and more severe. As they travelled down the Ucayali River, Ernesto spent most of his time lying in a hammock, cursing the mosquitoes and, as he wrote in his diary, staring 'dreamily out at the tempting jungle beyond the riverbank'.

Their immediate destination was the San Pablo **leper colony**, which they reached on 8 June. They stayed for twelve days, helping out where they could, and proving highly popular with the inmates. 'Their appreciation,' Ernesto wrote, 'stemmed from the fact that we didn't wear overalls or gloves, that we shook hands with them as we would the next man, sat with them, chatting about this and that, and played football with them. This may seem pointless bravado, but the psychological benefit to these poor people – usually treated like animals – of being treated as normal human beings is incalculable and the risk [of catching leprosy] incredibly remote.'

Leprosy

Leprosy is an infectious disease of the skin and nerve-ends which causes loss of sensation, nerve, organ and tissue damage, and obvious physical disfigurement. Over the centuries the disease has acquired a terrifying reputation, and until recently most people were unwilling to have anything to do with so-called 'lepers'. Most of those suffering from the disease were virtually imprisoned in out-of-the-way, isolated camps or 'leper colonies'. In recent years this situation has changed for the better, as more and more people have become aware that leprosy is not easy to catch.

Journey's end?

From San Pablo, Ernesto and Alberto rafted down the river to the Colombian port of Leticia, caught a plane to Bogotá, and then took buses to the Venezuelan capital, Caracas. There, after almost seven months together on the road, the two men parted company. Alberto headed off to his job in the leper

▶ *Ernesto (right) and Alberto Granado on a River Amazon raft in 1952.*

colony and Ernesto caught a ride on a Argentinian plane transporting horses to Miami. The plane was supposed to spend only one day on the ground in the USA before returning to Argentina, but a serious fault was discovered in one of the engines. Without any money, Ernesto found himself stranded in Miami for a month. He stayed with a cousin of Chichina's and spent most of his time on the beach.

He finally reached home on 31 August 1952. He had promised his mother that he would finish his medical studies, and he threw himself back into them, passing an astonishing fourteen exams in only a few months. He qualified as a doctor in July 1953. However, medicine no longer held enough of his interest. His trip with Alberto had opened his eyes to the enormous gulf between rich and poor which existed in South America, and shown him how medicine could achieve little in such a situation. People who lacked food, clothing and shelter, and who often worked long hours in dirty and dangerous conditions, would never be healthy. They needed a change in these conditions before they needed doctors.

The trip had also intensified his love of travel and his sense of adventure. He wanted more. Barely a month after qualifying as a doctor, Ernesto was on the move again, heading north with another friend from his school days, Carlos 'Calica' Ferrera. As their train pulled out of Buenos Aires' Retiro Station, Ernesto's weeping mother ran alongside, convinced that she would never see her favourite son again.

Guatemala and Fidel

Ernesto and Calica first stopped in Bolivia. A **revolution** had taken place there in April 1952 and Ernesto was eager to see how things had changed. But he was disappointed. The mines that supplied much of the country's wealth had been taken over by the state, and there had been limited **land reforms**, but the gap between rich and poor, powerful and powerless, had not been bridged. A few families still owned most of the fertile land, leaving the vast majority with either no land at all or small rocky plots. Ernesto saw Indian workers being badly treated by US supervisors, and watched peasants being sprayed with insecticide as they queued to see officials. This revolution, he decided, had not gone far enough.

▲ *Bolivian peasants at work on a terrace hillside in the Andes. The peasants' lives of poverty and abuse spurred Ernesto on in his fight for social change.*

FOR A MAP OF GUEVARA'S TRAVELS, SEE PAGE 12.

The two men travelled on across Peru, eventually reaching the port of Guayaquil in southern Ecuador. Here they ran into a group of travellers on their way to Guatemala in Central

Guatemala

In 1944, after many years of **dictatorship**, Guatemala enjoyed its first free elections. Successive governments led by presidents Arevalo and Arbenz introduced healthcare schemes in the cities, and laws to protect workers from being over-worked and under-paid on foreign-owned coffee and banana plantations. In 1952, Arbenz introduced a land reform which involved transferring land from the American-owned company United Fruit to poor peasants. Compensation was offered to the company, but it was declared inadequate by United Fruit and the US government. The dispute was reaching its climax when Ernesto Guevara arrived in Guatemala in December 1953.

America, where another revolution, or something very like one, seemed to be taking place. The **democratically elected** government led by President Jacob Arbenz had dared to challenge United Fruit, the all-powerful American company, which dominated the Guatemalan economy. Unlike the Bolivians, Arbenz was the sort of **revolutionary** that Ernesto appreciated. Ernesto decided that Venezuela and Alberto could wait. Parting company with Calica, he set out for Guatemala.

In the middle of a revolution

It took Ernesto two eventful months to reach Guatemala City. In Panama he was published for the first time – two travel articles on the ancient Inca settlement of Machu Picchu and Amazonia – and in Costa Rica he met a Peruvian revolutionary named Hilda Gadea. She introduced Ernesto to some Cuban revolutionaries, who told him about their leader Fidel Castro and how he had led an assault on the Cuban government's military barracks at Moncada in the previous June. The Cubans called Ernesto 'Che', the Argentinian word for 'buddy', often used by other Latin Americans when talking to Argentinians. The name stuck.

Ernesto reached Guatemala in the final days of 1953, and would remain there until the following August. Unable to practise as a doctor because he was a foreigner, he was forced to sell encyclopaedias and take on part-time work in a laboratory to earn a basic living. He suffered frequent **asthma** attacks. Despite all this, he was excited. He could have made money if he wanted – all he needed to do, he told his mother in a letter, was open a clinic specializing in **allergies**. But that, he wrote, 'would be the most horrible betrayal of the two "I"'s struggling inside me: the **socialist** and the traveller'. The socialist wanted to put the world to rights, the traveller wanted to see the world – and neither had time to run a clinic.

For the moment, the socialist was in control. He studied the writings of famous socialists and **communists**, and discussed politics endlessly with other revolutionaries. Hilda Gadea, who had also travelled to Guatemala, was now a close friend. She helped him through bouts of illness and introduced him to many people.

Meanwhile, US and Guatemalan business interests were growing increasingly afraid that the Guatemalan government's planned programme of social and economic reforms – which were intended to improve the conditions of ordinary Guatemalans – would greatly reduce business profits. They tried to persuade the government to think again, and when persuasion failed, they resorted to force. In June 1954, a US-sponsored invasion was launched and Guatemala City was bombed. Ernesto wrote that he 'thoroughly enjoyed himself' during these days of crisis, but also admitted to feeling a little ashamed of enjoying events in which many people were killed. But the excitement did not last long. Instead of putting up a fight, as Ernesto had hoped it would, the Arbenz government

▶ Guatemalan rebels in the town of Esquipilas during the American-sponsored invasion of 1954. Ernesto was disappointed that the Guatemalan government did not put up more of a fight against the invaders.

began to fall apart. Betrayed by its own army, the government refused to arm those who, like Ernesto, were willing to take on the invaders. By the end of June it had been overthrown, and Ernesto had become one of many revolutionaries who were forced to seek **asylum** in the Argentine embassy.

There he had several weeks to think about what had gone wrong. He had no doubt that Arbenz had been right to take on the USA because, as events had proved, that country would never willingly allow a revolution which threatened American business profits to succeed in **Latin America**. But Ernesto was equally certain that Arbenz should have created a revolutionary army for the protection of his revolutionary government. And he should not have allowed the opposition so much freedom, particularly in the press, to criticize his revolution, because that had weakened and undermined the resistance to American pressure. When the time came in Cuba, Ernesto would remember these lessons.

Ready for action

Ernesto eventually moved on to Mexico, and for a while made a living photographing American tourists before finding some part-time research work studying allergies. He had a good apartment, ate well, and even took a bath every day. His friendship with Hilda turned into a romance.

FOR DETAILS ON KEY PEOPLE OF GUEVARA'S TIME, SEE PAGE 58.

However, there was no lessening of his anger. He believed that the events he had witnessed in Guatemala had proved him right, and wrote to his mother of his 'growing indignation' at the way in which the 'gringos' (white foreigners) treated Latin America. He was ready for action, ready for the chance to fight which he had been denied in Guatemala.

In the summer of 1955, Ernesto met Fidel Castro, the leader of the failed assault on the Moncada barracks and of the Cuban 26 July Movement, named after the date on which the assault took place. The two men hit it off immediately, and when Castro invited Ernesto to join his seaborne assault on the Cuban government as the expedition's doctor, Ernesto agreed.

That same summer he married Hilda, who was now pregnant. Their daughter, Hildita, was born in February 1956, but there was no possibility

▲ *An early photo of the guerrillas in the jungle. Guevara is second from left, and Castro stands in the centre with his brother Raul kneeling in front of him.*

Fidel Castro

Fidel Castro was nearing his twenty-ninth birthday when he first met
Guevara in the summer of 1955. Born in Cuba's Oriente province, Castro
had studied and practised law in the early 1950s, before deciding to
concentrate on politics. When Fulgencio Batista seized power in 1952,
destroying Cuban democracy and setting himself up as a dictator, Castro
organized and led an assault on Santiago de Cuba's Moncada military
barracks on 26 July 1953. The assault failed, and Castro received a long
prison sentence, but was released as part of a general **amnesty** in the
summer of 1955. Moving to Mexico, Castro set about forming his
26 July Movement which, less than four years later, would drive
Batista from Cuba.

▶ *Hilda Gadea in London in 1969, two years after*
Guevara's murder in captivity.

that Ernesto would settle for life with this
new family. He had already found another
family which was more important to him,
the family of revolutionaries.

Throughout 1956, the preparations for
Castro's assault went on. In the Cuban
guerrillas' training camp Ernesto finally
became known simply as 'Che'. Despite his
illness, he regularly came first in all the
keep-fit and other military training exercises, and by the end
of the year he had repeatedly demonstrated that he was
much more than just the expedition's doctor. When the boat
which Castro had purchased, the *Granma*, finally sailed for
Cuba in December 1956, Che Guevara, the only non-Cuban
on board, was already one of Fidel Castro's right-hand men.

Comandante!

The journey to Cuba was supposed to take five days, but it took seven. There were eighty-two men on a boat with room for twenty, and most of them were seasick. A faulty clutch slowed the craft down, and half the supplies were washed overboard in a storm. The *Granma* finally reached the Cuban coast two days late and at the wrong destination. Its passengers were forced to spend several hours cutting their way through a mangrove swamp before they finally reached dry land.

FOR A MAP OF GUEVARA'S TRAVELS, SEE PAGE 12.

The exhausted and hungry men were soon betrayed to the authorities by one of the guides sent to meet them by local supporters. Three days after the landing, they were suddenly attacked by Batista's soldiers and planes in the sugarcane fields of Alegría del Pío. By the end of that day, the twenty or so survivors were stumbling through the night in the general direction of Cuba's highest mountains, the Sierra Maestra. The Cuban **Revolution** had got off to a bad start.

The first few weeks

Che Guevara was shot in the neck at Alegría del Pío. The amount of blood pouring from the wound convinced him that he was about to die. For a few seconds he just sat there, remembering how a character in a book he had read had calmly leaned back against a tree and died in a dignified manner. But one of his fellow **guerrillas** rudely interrupted him, shouting that he should get moving, and Che found that he was not dying after all. The wound looked a lot worse than it was.

◀ *The Cuban dictator Fulgencio Batista, who was overthrown by the army of the 26 July Movement.*

▶ *A Cuban poster of the 1960s featuring heroes of the revolution. Che, cigar in mouth, sits below Fidel Castro and above Camilo Cienfuegos.*

Around two weeks later, his small group met up with the other surviving fighters – who included Fidel Castro, his brother Raul, and the popular Camilo Cienfuegos – in the foothills of the mountains. Fidel wasted no time in announcing their survival. In mid-January 1957 they attacked a small military post, capturing weapons and regaining the confidence they had lost in those disastrous first few days. Soon new recruits and fresh supplies were on their way to the mountains from 26 July Movement supporters in Cuba's towns. More small **skirmishes** with the army followed, but already the local **peasants** were siding with the guerrillas, sharing their knowledge of the countryside and warning of army movements.

In late January, during a skirmish in a gorge called Hell's Ravine, Che killed one of Batista's soldiers with a rifle shot. It was the first time he had killed a man. A few weeks later he ordered – and, according to some accounts, carried out – the execution of a fellow guerrilla, Eutimio, who had tried to betray the group to the authorities. In these first weeks of the **revolutionary** war he discovered that he was able to turn off his emotions and be utterly ruthless if he was convinced that the situation required it. In addition, despite repeated **asthma** attacks, he toured the local villages with his doctor's bag and whatever medicines he could lay his hands on.

His own command

Che got on well with Castro. They respected each other, and found that they could argue without creating any lasting ill will. In May the guerrillas successfully attacked a small military post at El Uvero, with Che leading bravely from the front. After this victory Castro split his army, now 200 strong, into two, and appointed Che commander – *comandante* – of the 75-strong second column. According to Che, 'the dose of vanity that we all have inside made me feel the proudest man on earth.'

Che and his men fought several successful skirmishes against Batista's army during that summer and autumn, and set up their own base at El Hombrito in the Sierra Maestra, which included a bread oven, a newspaper printing press, a simple hospital and a weapons store. Che also organized classes teaching his soldiers and the local villagers how to read and write.

FOR A MAP OF IMPORTANT CUBAN SITES, SEE PAGE 28.

A hard man to follow

Che was earning something of a reputation among his troops. He was well-organized, clever, and courageous to the point of foolhardiness – after he was shot in the foot in December 1957, Castro scolded him for taking too many risks.

◀ *Che in the central Cuban town of Santa Clara, soon after its capture by his column in December 1958.*

He accepted no privileges of rank; on the contrary, he insisted on receiving exactly the same treatment as everyone else. He queued for food like all the others, and took the same portions. Such behaviour won him the lifelong loyalty of many who fought with him, and several would later follow him to their deaths in Bolivia.

However, there was a darker side to this fierce insistence on shared discipline and equality. Che was a bad man to cross. He was ruthless to traitors, and he refused to make allowances for others' weaknesses. He never asked anyone to do anything that he was not prepared to do himself, but he did insist that everyone else live up to his own extraordinary standards. Since few men were as courageous, intelligent or determined as he was, he was often disappointed.

▶ *Fidel Castro and Che Guevara in the Sierra Maestra mountains of Cuba, early in the revolutionary war.*

Friendly encouragement

'We [Che and his fellow-guerrilla, Crespo] had to move fast to reach the hillside and cross to the other side before the troops cut us off, but it was not difficult because we had seen them in time.... Everybody made it to the top, but for me it was a terrible experience. I was practically choking by the time I reached the top of the hill. I remember Crespo's efforts to make me walk. Every time I said I could not go on and asked to be left behind, Crespo would revert to our jargon and snap at me: "You, son-of-a-bitch from Argentina, either you walk or I'll hit you with my rifle butt!"'

Che Guevara, writing in *The Revolutionary War*. He was suffering badly from asthma at the time of this skirmish.

The final push

In the early summer of 1958, Batista launched a great offensive against the revolutionaries in the Sierra Maestra, deploying 10,000 reluctant troops against the 300 or so guerrillas. It was a disaster. Batista's soldiers were unable to find the guerrillas, but every now and then the guerrillas found them. By August, 1,000 troops had been killed or wounded, and 400 taken prisoner. It was the beginning of the end for Batista's **dictatorship**.

▼ A map of Cuba, showing the locations at which important events occurred during Che's involvement with the island.

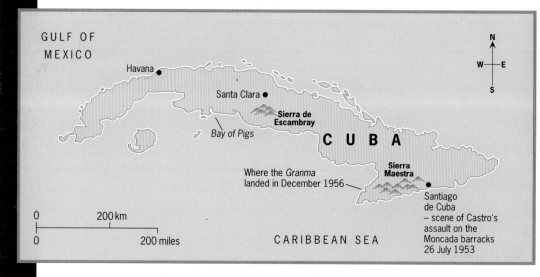

Castro decided it was time for the guerrillas to leave their mountain nests, and that summer he ordered Che and Camilo Cienfuegos to lead two columns up the island to a new base in the Sierra de Escambray. It took 46 days for Che's 148 men to march the 300 kilometres, battling constantly against mosquitoes, cyclones, hunger, and those remnants of Batista's army and airforce that still had the will to fight.

Nevertheless, by mid-October the rebels were firmly established in the centre of the island, and Batista's control was fast slipping away. During this period, Che met a young woman called Aleida March who was working as a **courier** between the rebel armies and their supporters in the towns. The sixth daughter of a local farmer, she would become his second wife in June of the following year, after his divorce from Hilda.

By late December, the town of Santa Clara was all that stood between Che and the open road to Havana, Cuba's capital. His men were outnumbered by at least ten to one, but Batista's soldiers had little interest in fighting, and were counting on a train carrying reinforcements that had been sent from Havana. Once this had been derailed by the rebels, the soldiers surrendered in droves. The revolutionaries had won the war.

Falling in love

Early in the battle for the town of Santa Clara, Aleida left Che's side to dash across a street under fire. For a few seconds she was out of sight, and he wasn't sure if she had made it safely to the other side. In those few seconds, he said later, he realized that he was in love with her.

◀ *Che during the battle of Santa Clara.*

Falling out with the USA

Once in Havana, Che was put in command of La Cabaña fortress, which had served the Batista **regime** as a barracks, weapons store and prison. He was given the job of rounding up those responsible for atrocities and war crimes committed by Batista's supporters during his years in power. After the battle of Santa Clara, Che had ordered the execution of several torturers, and many new graves containing Batista's victims were discovered in the early months of peace. Many of those responsible were tried and executed at La Cabaña. Their trials were probably less than fair, but the eventual execution of around 550 people was generally welcomed by the vast majority of the Cuban people. Many of the wealthy and privileged, who had supported and benefited from the Batista regime but were not considered guilty of specific crimes against the people, were allowed to leave Cuba, mostly for the USA.

Che also had several personal matters to deal with. Hilda arrived in Cuba with their daughter Hildita, only to discover that Che had fallen in love with Aleida. Hilda reluctantly agreed to give him a divorce. Che made an effort to establish a relationship with Hildita: during January 1959 Che and his three-year-old daughter were often seen walking around La Cabaña fortress hand in hand.

◀ Fidel and Che reviewing a military parade in Cuba in August 1960.

That same month, Che's mother, father, sisters and younger brother arrived from Argentina to see him. He took them on a quick tour of the island, and showed them some of the sights of the **revolutionary** war. He told them he had no intention of returning either to medicine or to Argentina.

Making victory count

In mid-January, Che suffered a severe **asthma** attack, probably brought on by the combined stresses of his work at La Cabaña and the difficulties of his family life. He was sent to recover in a house by the sea at Tarará, some 20 kilometres from Havana. Here, over a period of several weeks, he took a leading part in a series of unofficial gatherings at which several of Cuba's new leaders discussed the future of their **revolution**. Che was always in favour of the most far-reaching policies, like greater equality of wages, more long-term economic planning by government, a widespread government takeover of industries and services, and **land reform** which involved breaking up all the large estates.

The revolutionaries had brought down Batista's government, he argued, but how were they to improve the lives of ordinary Cubans? They could only do this if they also destroyed the social and economic systems – the patterns of ownership and control (who owned what, who ran what) – that Batista had supported, and which were still supported by rich Cubans and the USA. Such a programme would provoke great opposition, both inside and outside Cuba. The new Cuba therefore needed an efficient **security police** to reduce opposition to the new regime, and an army that was completely loyal to the new government. The country required radical **agrarian reform**, partly because the ordinary people needed more land, and partly because the few rich people who owned most of the land had supported Batista. Taking land away from the rich would reduce their power to oppose the revolution.

In Che's view, the country also had to move beyond its reliance on sugar production, which accounted for 40 per cent of the national income and 80 per cent of its exports. Cuba should diversify its economy by creating industries in the towns and growing a much wider variety of crops in the countryside.

Che was not a member of the **Communist** Party, but he considered himself a communist. Believing, as he did, that the 26 July Movement and the Cuban Communist Party had similar goals, he encouraged them to work together. He also hoped that Cuba would draw closer to the Soviet Union, the only country that could remotely match the power of the USA. The first, overwhelmingly popular agrarian reform of May 1959 met with violent opposition from the USA. The reform offered what the Americans considered inadequate compensation for its confiscation of large sugar and rice plantations. For Cuba, it made the need for friends seem even more urgent. Che was convinced that sooner or later the Cuban Revolution would face the same sort of US invasion that had toppled President Jacob Arbenz in Guatemala.

Ambassador and banker

In June, only ten days after his marriage to Aleida, Che set out on a three-month world tour to gather support for the revolution. He visited many countries – Egypt, Japan, Yugoslavia, India, Sri Lanka,

◀ *Che and his second wife Aleida leave for their honeymoon in June 1959.*

Indonesia, Pakistan, Sudan and Morocco – and talked with many of the **developing world**'s leading statesmen. With some he was refreshingly honest: when Egypt's President Nasser told Che that only a few Egyptians had fled the country after their revolution, he replied that if this was the case it couldn't have been much of a revolution. But with others he showed an acute lack of political experience: in Indonesia he was completely taken in by President Sukarno, mistaking the corrupt **dictator** for a model developing world leader. Seeing what he wanted to see was always one of Che's greatest weaknesses.

▲ *Che, the roving ambassador: meeting with Egypt's President Nasser in July 1959.*

Before leaving Cuba, Che had been put in charge of the Industrial Department of the National Institute of Agrarian Reform (INRA), and on his return in September 1959 he resumed his work supervising the re-structuring of the sugar industry, Cuba's most important resource. A few weeks later, he was also appointed Director of the National Bank, which put him in charge of the currency and Cuba's finances, both internally and externally. Castro knew that Che had no great knowledge of economics, but he trusted him more than many of those who had, and he had great faith in Che's organizational skills. Fourteen months later, Che left the Bank to become Minister of Industry, another key economic job. For about four years, from mid-1959 to mid-1963, he was the man responsible for running Cuba's economy.

FOR DETAILS ON KEY PEOPLE OF GUEVARA'S TIME, SEE PAGE 58.

Che brought enthusiasm and apparently limitless energy to the task. He did his best to learn economics. Perhaps most importantly, he brought a sense of discipline and organizational ability to the early years of the Cuban Revolution, qualities that had traditionally been easier to find in his native Argentina than in easy-going Cuba. Although he gave the impression that he spent most of his time at the Bank with his feet up on the desk, chatting to friends and smoking cigars, he got the work done, and saw that others did too. Signing Cuban banknotes 'Che' seemed casual, and almost disrespectful, but the point he was making was that bank presidents were no more important than sugarcane cutters or mechanics.

A life of work

His official jobs were only part of the story. In November 1959, Che helped start the Volunteer Work Programme. This involved citizens giving up evenings or parts of their weekends to work on projects such as building a school or cutting sugarcane. Doing such jobs in a spirit of common purpose made people aware of what they were all doing for each other, and strengthened their sense of community. It was important that the leaders set an example, and Che happily gave up most of his Saturdays to do volunteer work.

There were also government affairs to attend to, speeches to give and talks with the many foreigners who came to Cuba eager to learn about the revolution. Che spent many evenings writing *Guerrilla Warfare*, a manual for those who he hoped would follow in Cuba's footsteps. All this work left little time for family life. He and Aleida lived in a small, comfortable, but far from luxurious house in Havana's Nevado Vedado quarter. Though different in many ways – his idea of fun was reading, hers was going out – the two of them were still in love, and, late in 1960, their first child was born. She was named after her mother, and known as Aleidita. His former wife Hilda had also settled down in Havana and his daughter Hildita usually stayed with her father and Aleida at weekends.

Che could have filled his home with the gifts he was always receiving on his foreign trips, but he gave all these away to youth training centres. Neither would he let Aleida take advantage of his position. When she wanted to take the children to school in his government car, he insisted that she take the bus, 'like everyone else'.

◀ *Che sets an example, doing voluntary work in the early years of the revolution.*

The Bay of Pigs

By this time, the disputes between Cuba and the USA had snowballed into a full-scale crisis. In 1960, the USA first reduced the amount of Cuban sugar it was buying, and then stopped buying it altogether, acts that threatened enormous damage to Cuba's economic prospects. Fortunately for Cuba, help was available. The **Cold War** conflict between the USA and the Soviet Union, which had acquired a new and dangerous edge in the late 1950s, meant that the Soviets were happy to help any enemies of the USA. They agreed to buy Cuba's sugar.

US-Cuban relations grew more hostile. When US-owned oil refineries in Cuba refused to refine oil which Cuba had bought from the Soviet Union, the Cuban government took

them over. The USA responded with an economic **embargo** – banning trade between Cuba and the USA in everything but food and medicines. The Cubans then nationalized (took into state ownership) a further 166 American companies, and forged a closer bond with the Soviet Union. In October 1960, Che led the first official Cuban mission to Moscow.

◀ *Fidel, Che and a visitor from the Soviet Union, Deputy-Premier Anastas Mikoyan.*

Che's hope

'The only privileged people in Cuba will be the children.'
(Che Guevara, in 1961, claiming that children, and only children,
would be put first in the new Cuba.)

Throughout the year, anti-revolutionary Cuban **exiles** (people who had fled to the USA from Cuba when the Batista regime fell), financed and supported by US intelligence agencies, continued a campaign of **sabotage** and **terrorism** against the island. It seemed only a matter of time before the USA invaded. Finally, in April 1961, an army of 1500 exiles, supported by American planes flying out of Nicaragua, landed at a bay on Cuba's southern shore known as Playa Giron, or the Bay of Pigs. The Cuban army and people, whom Castro had armed to defend their still overwhelmingly popular revolution, swiftly defeated it.

Che was not involved in the fighting, but he was wounded nevertheless. Placed in charge of the western portion of the island, he accidentally shot himself in the cheek when he dropped a gun. Had he been holding the gun at a slightly different angle, he would have killed himself. As it was, he spent a day in hospital and several more recovering from the injury.

In one sense, though, he was a happy man. The Bay of Pigs invasion had proved him right: the USA had shown itself to be a determined enemy of the Cuban Revolution. It was time to choose sides once and for all, and to take Cuba into the **communist bloc**.

Cuba's victory at the Bay of Pigs offered vivid proof of the continuing popularity of the **revolution** and its leaders, but that popularity was about to be tested to the limit. The Cuban economy that Che presided over was heading into a nosedive. Shortages were becoming increasingly common, and early in 1962 **rationing** was introduced for a long list of basic goods, including rice, beans, eggs, milk, toothpaste and detergent. What had gone wrong?

Reasons for economic failure

The virtual collapse of the Cuban economy was partly a result of the dispute with its northern neighbour. Before the revolution, Cuba had bought nearly everything from the USA, and had sold almost everything to it. Now it had to find new markets in which to buy and sell. There was also the problem of finding spare parts for all those American goods and machines which had been bought in the past.

Not everything could be blamed on the US **embargo**, however. The Cubans, and Che, had made serious mistakes of their own, some for the best of motives, others out of sheer inexperience. For example, too much had been spent on huge increases in healthcare and education for ordinary people. There was no doubt that Cuba needed better healthcare and education – they were what the revolution was all about – but the country could not really afford them.

More damagingly, the attempt to lessen Cuba's dependence on sugar, to grow other crops and to create new industries, had been badly planned and overambitious. The sugar harvest had certainly been reduced, but the money lost in sugar sales had not been made up in other ways, so there was less to spend on the raw materials needed for the new industries. Clearly, the Cubans and Che were beginners when it came to planning an economy, and they were trying to do too much too soon.

They hoped for help from the Soviet Union, both in expertise and equipment. But the quality of help they received was much poorer, and the price much higher, than they had expected. To make matters even worse, it soon became apparent that the Soviets expected more than money for their assistance: they also demanded a say in how the assistance was used. Between 1961 and 1964, Che's work in Cuba was dominated by his growing disillusion with the Soviets, from whom he had once expected so much.

▼ *In New York, Cuban* **exiles** *demonstrate against the Castro* **regime**. *Many wealthy landowners, businessmen, scientists, engineers, teachers, doctors, artists and writers fled to the USA in the 1950s. Their departure badly affected the Cuban economy.*

Two ways forward

Gradually, during these years, Che realized that Cuba was faced with a very basic choice – it could do things the Soviet way, or it could do things his way. As far as Cuba was concerned, the Soviet way meant relying on sugar, on producing and selling as much as it could to other **communist** countries, and using the money earned to pay for clinics and schools and a few new industries.

In return for its guarantee to buy all the sugar Cuba could produce, the Soviet Union demanded something in return – political loyalty. The Cubans would be required to organize their society along Soviet lines, introducing economic reforms

▼ *The Soviet leader Nikita Khrushchev at a press conference in 1959.*

that the Soviet leader Khrushchev and his successors were introducing in the Soviet Union, reforms which involved greater rewards for the best-run enterprises and higher wages for the most valuable workers. Cuba was also expected to support the Soviet policy of '**peaceful co-existence**' with the USA. It was not to offer any help to other armed revolutions, in **Latin America** or elsewhere.

FOR DETAILS ON KEY PEOPLE OF GUEVARA'S TIME, SEE PAGE 58.

Che's priorities were very different. For a start, he thought the Soviets should be much more generous in their dealings with **developing** countries like Cuba. They should not, in fact, treat them in much the same way as a **capitalist** country would, demanding the highest prices they could. More importantly, he was increasingly opposed to Soviet policies, both at home and abroad. For Che, giving people more money for working harder was a betrayal of **communism**. He wanted to pay all workers much the same, and to rely on enthusiasm and will power to make them work harder.

Such a programme, he believed, would create the conditions for both economic and political success. After all, **socialism** and communism were about more than raising the material standing of living. They were also about creating the 'new man' or person, who was motivated by love of his/her fellow human beings and a sense of duty, not by greed.

A lost battle

In the autumn of 1962, the Cuban Missile Crisis erupted. Although it had no real relevance to the economic and political future of the Cuban Revolution, it certainly increased Che's disillusionment with the Soviet Union. Until then, he had been all in favour of placing Soviet missiles in Cuba – 'anything that can stop the Americans is worthwhile,' he said.

▲ *President John F. Kennedy (centre) meets with US army officials during the Cuban Missile Crisis of 1962.*

Che was furious when Khrushchev, under intense pressure from US President John F. Kennedy, agreed to remove the missiles. Che's anger helps to explain some of his more extreme statements at this time, like his claim that the Cuban people were 'prepared to be atomically incinerated so that their ashes may be used as the foundations of new societies'. Che was assuming that everyone else was prepared to make the same sacrifices as he was: as was usually the case, this assumption was quite wrong.

Castro was also furious with the Soviets, but he knew that Cuba was ultimately dependent on their help and good will. In economic matters, his heart agreed with Che, but his head told him that the Soviet way was the only practical solution. In the spring of 1963, Castro spent more than a month in the Soviet Union, arguing for the best deal he could get. In January 1964, a long-term agreement was signed. Cuba would limit itself to sugar and other agricultural production for sale in the Soviet Union and Eastern Europe, and would receive industrial

The Cuban Missile Crisis

In 1962, the Soviet Union supplied Cuba with nuclear missiles which, they claimed, were for its defence following the Bay of Pigs invasion. The USA objected to the siting of these missiles so close its shores. It imposed a **naval blockade** around Cuba to prevent the delivery of any more missiles, and demanded that the Soviets withdraw those that were already there. Threatened with the possibility of a nuclear war, the Soviets backed down. Without consulting the Cubans, they agreed to withdraw the missiles in exchange for America's promise not to invade Cuba.

goods in return. The Cuban communists would have to fit in and do what they were told. Che had lost his battle for a different way of building communism in Cuba, and he knew it.

Time to leave?

Che continued to write articles and address meetings around the world, hoping to inspire both present and future generations with his vision and determination. Yet during 1964 his thoughts turned increasingly away from the battle he felt he had lost in Cuba, towards the battles that might still be won elsewhere in the world.

Key dates of the Cuban Revolution

1956	• November	The *Granma* sails for Cuba
1959	• January	The victorious army of the 26 July Movement enters Havana
1959–1960		Series of increasingly bitter disputes between Cuba and the USA
1961	• April	US-supported invasion of Cuba lands in the Bay of Pigs
1962	• October	The Cuban Missile Crisis
1963–1964		Cuba's economic ties with the Soviet Union are strengthened
1965	• April	Che Guevara leaves Cuba, having given up all his official jobs

Che was faced with a difficult decision. It was difficult to imagine leaving Fidel, whom he still loved and respected despite their differences. He said at this point that he found it hard to imagine either marriage or divorce where Fidel was concerned; he could neither stay with his old friend nor leave him. Then there was his family. He and Aleida now had three children: Aleidita, their first son Camilo, born in May 1962, and second daughter Celia, born in June 1963. And he was still immensely popular among the Cuban people, who had taken the Argentinian to their hearts and kept him there, despite the economic failures. Yet, in the end, he had to go.

Where should Che go to start a new **revolution**? He was naturally drawn towards **Latin America**, but there were good reasons for looking elsewhere. For one thing, the Americans were likely to take Cuban interference in Latin America very seriously. For another, most Latin American **communist** parties obediently followed the Soviet line that power should be won politically, and not through waging a **guerrilla** war in the countryside. If Che did start such a war somewhere in Latin America, then the Soviets would see to it that he received little help from the cities, where most Communist Party members lived.

Choosing the Congo

Che needed to find somewhere more remote from American and Soviet influence. He looked to Africa, touring the continent in December 1964 and January 1965. He met with leaders who had recently won independence from the old **colonial** powers, and saw as much as he could of how ordinary people lived their lives. He was moved by the degrees of poverty and **oppression** he witnessed, and persuaded himself that he could do something about it. The Republic of the Congo, in

▲ *Che pictured here with his son Camilo.*

FOR DETAILS ON KEY PEOPLE OF GUEVARA'S TIME, SEE PAGE 58.

particular, caught his attention. A revolution seemed to be already underway in this huge country at the heart of Africa; if successful, it might spill across its borders and set the whole continent ablaze.

Back in Cuba, Che persuaded Fidel to allow him to lead a small force of Cuban soldiers to the Congo. Che's wife, Aleida, had just given birth to their second son Ernesto (born on 24 February 1965), and was upset at his leaving, but this second marriage, like the first, was less important to Che than his sense of personal mission. If he did not come back, he told her, she should remarry.

Problems, problems

Che arrived in Tanzania in mid-April 1965 with the first of the 130 Cubans selected for the expedition – almost all of them Afro-Cubans, since it was felt that Africans might see white Cubans as new colonialists. A few days later, Che and his soldiers crossed Lake Tanganyika and set up camp on the Congolese side, in the village of Kibamba. This was in territory controlled by the Congolese rebels led by Laurent Kabila, who were fighting to overthrow the pro-Western government of Moise Tshombe. Kibamba would be Che's headquarters for seven intensely frustrating months.

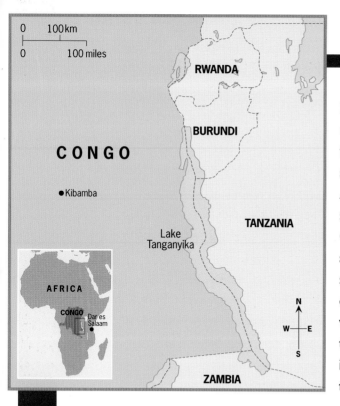

▲ A map showing where Che and his small group of men tried to start a revolution in Africa.

In the Congo, Che was in charge of his small Cuban force, but he had no authority over anyone else. At the beginning, this seemed only right. It was a Congolese **revolution**, he argued, and the Congolese should be giving the military orders. He and his Cubans were there to help train the locals, to support them in action if necessary, but not to do their fighting for them.

However, the Congolese leaders, like Laurent Kabila, understood the situation better than Che. They knew that the revolution had very little chance of success, and preferred living comfortable lives in exile rather than organizing any fighting. Left to fend for themselves in the camps, their troops drank, fought among themselves, and intimidated the local **peasants**. They explained to their astonished Cuban trainers that they were protected by *dawa*, a magical belief in the power of a potion that, once rubbed over their bodies, would protect them from bullets.

Che also had personal problems to deal with. The climate was terrible for his **asthma**, and he suffered frequent attacks, losing almost a quarter of his body weight. At the end of May he received news from Cuba that his mother was dying in Argentina. His family had tried to reach him earlier, but his

presence in Africa was still supposed to be a secret, and his
mother died without knowing why he had not come to her
or sent word.

Defeat

When Kabila finally ordered his forces to attack a government
stronghold, it proved disastrous. Many of the Congolese
troops ran away the moment they came under fire, and four
of the Cubans accompanying them were killed. The Cubans'
presence in Africa was now known, and the Congolese
government ordered its powerful army of white
mercenaries to drive them out. Che's troops enjoyed one
successful ambush in July, but their situation deteriorated
sharply during the next few months.

In November, a change in the Congolese government
persuaded Tanzania and other African countries to end their
support for the rebellion. Without this support, Che and his
men could not continue. The Cubans withdrew across the
lake to Tanzania, and the men were flown home. Weak and
dispirited, Che spent several months recovering his strength,
first in the Tanzanian capital Dar es Salaam, and then in
Prague, the capital of communist Czechoslovakia. What was
he to do now?

The Republic of the Congo

During its first five years of independence (1960–5) the former
Belgian Congo witnessed the murder of one prime minister (Patrice
Lumumba), and a failed attempt by the richest province (Katanga)
to gain its own independence. It also saw the arrival and departure
of a United Nations peacekeeping force, and armed uprisings in
many different parts of the country. The Congo seemed, in many
ways, ripe for revolution. However, by the time Che reached the
Republic in the spring of 1965, most of the rebellious activity had
been brought under control by government-hired white mercenary
troops. He was, as the Algerian leader Ben Bella said, 'too late'.

Death in Bolivia

Following the defeat in Africa, Che's first instinct was to make Argentina his next target. Castro believed that this would be little more than a suicide mission, and tried to persuade Che that Bolivia was a better bet. In Bolivia, Castro and others argued, the countryside was better suited to **guerrilla warfare**. There was a strong **left-wing** tradition, and recruits would be easier to find for the guerrilla army. Like the Congo, Bolivia sat at the heart of a huge landmass, and could be used as a base for **revolutionary** action in many other countries, including, in the long run, Argentina.

Beaten before he began

Che allowed himself to be persuaded, and in July 1966 he returned to Cuba for the last time. During the next three months, he selected and prepared the mixed Cuban-Bolivian

▼ *Surrounded by local people, Che (seated, on the right) studies a map during the final weeks of his war in Bolivia.*

Saying his goodbyes

In October 1966, Che said goodbye to Aleida, and to their four children. Heavily disguised for his trip to Bolivia – with his hair plucked out to make him appear bald, and wearing a suit, tie and glasses – he introduced himself to the children as their 'Uncle Ramon', and told them how much their father loved them.

At the training camp Che had shared a long farewell conversation with Fidel Castro, the two men sitting side by side on a log. Castro tried to persuade Che to postpone the operation, but he failed. They hugged each other, and then sat together for a long time in silence.

team who would fight under him in Bolivia. He lived at a training camp in the mountains, where Aleida often came to visit him.

Late in October 1966, Che travelled to Bolivia. Two possible locations had been suggested for a guerrilla base. Under pressure from the Bolivian **Communist** Party and its leader Mario Monje, Che selected Ñancahuazú, the one closest to Argentina. The other location offered better cover for guerrilla activity and a larger population from which to draw recruits, but the Bolivian Communist Party, despite its stated eagerness to help, was anxious to steer Che away from its own territory.

Upon reaching Ñancahuazú, Che had good reason to be depressed. There were only a few men waiting for him, a small quantity of weapons, and little medicine or food. In December, Mario Monje arrived at the camp to demand the final say in any action proposed by Che and his soldiers. Che, mindful of what had happened in Africa, refused to surrender his leadership.

From this point on, Monje and the Bolivian Communist Party were more of a hindrance than a help, actively campaigning to prevent Bolivian sympathizers from joining the guerrillas. Che's army, little more than thirty strong at this point, was never to grow much bigger.

Slide to disaster

In February 1967, an undeterred Che led his men out on a reconnaissance march (recce) around the local area. It was supposed to last two weeks, but it took six. Two men drowned in swollen rivers; the thorny vegetation ripped the clothes and boots of the other men to shreds, and serious insect bites covered their skin. Hungry and thirsty, Che's soldiers were reduced to angry bickering and near **mutiny** before they had even faced a human enemy.

The men returned to Ñancahuazú to find that the Bolivian army had discovered their base, and were waiting for their return. Che managed to organize a successful ambush of the army unit concerned, but he might have done better just to walk away. Now the authorities were certain that a real threat existed, and the guerrillas had no hope of recruiting new fighters, creating a network of supporters in the city, or talking to the outside world. They were on their own.

Che split his force in two, hoping to recombine them at a later date, but the two columns never saw each other again. Hunted by the Bolivian army, they marched around the area looking for each other, stopping to occupy a village or two, but never feeling strong enough to attack a military target. There was no help from the local peasants, no help from the cities, and none from Cuba – the Soviets had warned Castro that they would cut off their crucial economic aid to Cuba if he defied their policy of not supporting armed struggles and went to Che's assistance.

The end

Weakened by **asthma** attacks and stomach problems, Che struggled on. At the end of August, the second column of soldiers was ambushed crossing a river, and most of its members were killed. In early October, Che's own column was finally trapped in the Yuro Ravine. Wounded in the leg and unable to walk, he also found that his gun had jammed.

Che was taken as a prisoner to the schoolhouse of a nearby town, La Higuera. His captors, not knowing what to do with him, asked their superiors for instructions. The following morning, 9 October 1967, orders arrived from the capital. The soldiers guarding him drew lots, and the man selected to perform the execution pumped half a dozen bullets into the helpless Che as he lay on the schoolhouse floor.

▼ *Che's dead body, laid out in the hospital morgue at Vallegrande and surrounded by members of the Bolivian Armed Forces.*

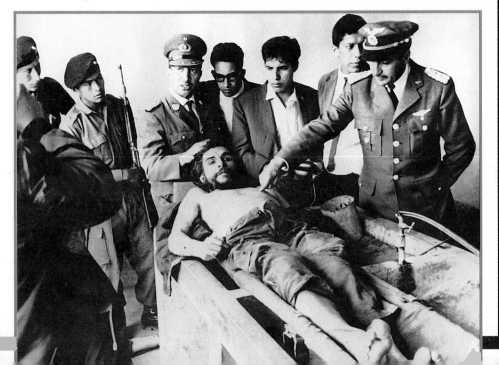

Che once told his children that he hoped imperialism – the exploitation of poor countries by richer ones – would be gone by the end of the twentieth century. In this, as in so much else, his dreams were not to be realized. More than thirty years have passed since his death, and the system he fought against seems as strong as ever. The gap between rich and poor has, if anything, widened. The solutions to the social and political injustices he witnessed in **Latin America** and Africa are as hard to find now as they were then.

The style of **guerrilla warfare** he practised, wrote about and championed has proved a costly and dismal failure in many places where it has been tried. Although the kind of **communism** he came to despise in the Soviet Union has all but vanished, the type of communism he hoped to build in Cuba and elsewhere

◀ *A statue of Che Guevara holding a child in Santa Clara, Cuba.*

has proved an elusive and, many would say, impractical dream. His beloved Cuban **Revolution**, battered by decades of Soviet blackmail and American bullying, is no longer the inspiration it once was.

Successes and failures

Che's contributions to the success of the Cuban **revolutionary** war – his physical courage, his intelligence, his vision – were enormous. He helped give the Cuban Revolution that heady mixture of youth, idealism and absolute determination that characterized its early years. As long as Che had any say in the matter, there was no back-sliding on their promises to the Cuban people, no surrender to the revolution's enemies.

In his work, personal style and writings he gave the Cuban Revolution something different, something with a romantic appeal that reached way beyond Cuba. He was a **communist**, but a communist who seemed different to those in power elsewhere. Unlike them, he said what he thought, and seemed motivated by a genuine and selfless desire to build a better, fairer world.

When Che failed, it was usually because he was attempting the impossible. He spent his life fighting the crippling affliction of his **asthma**. This reckless refusal to accept his own shortcomings, in this and other matters, was little short of heroic, but a similar intolerance of the shortcomings of others made him sometimes behave, as he himself admitted, in an almost cruel way. His major failures – with the Cuban economy, and in Africa and Bolivia – were critically affected by this intolerance of the failings of other people.

The way to communism

Che's most important legacy was probably his contribution to **socialist** and communist thought. The story of the twentieth century was largely the story of communism's rise and fall, and Che's own story was very much a part of this. His faith in Soviet communism soon diminished once he had witnessed the way it really worked, and in his final years he talked and wrote a great deal about creating a better, more human form of communism.

▼ *Thousands wave flags and lift portraits during Che's official funeral on 17 October 1997, almost thirty years after his death.*

Like two other leading twentieth century figures with whom he had little else in common – Mahatma Gandhi and Martin Luther King Jr. – Che Guevara realized that the way in which you go about getting something affects what you get. Just as Gandhi and King believed that social harmony could never be achieved through violence, so Che believed that communism could never be created with capitalist methods. If a government appealed only to the greed of its citizens – as the Soviet government was increasingly doing in the 1960s – it would never end up with a society in which people cared for one another. Communism, Che believed, had first and foremost to find a place in people's hearts. If it did that, then the social benefits would automatically follow.

Self-sacrifice

Finally, and most obviously, Che's life and death have come to represent an example to others. As he saw it, the point of life was to help others less fortunate than himself, and he lived accordingly. There was, of course, a wilful, selfish streak in all this: Che's untiring pursuit of his own political ideals was undoubtedly hard for those closest to him.

However, in a world that seems increasingly obsessed with personal pleasure and enrichment, it is hard to be entirely critical of someone whose life was driven by his hatred of injustice. As Che himself wrote, in his last letter to his family: 'Many will call me an adventurer, and I am, but of a different kind – one who risks his skin to prove his convictions.'

The legend

'For millions of the dispossessed [those who had been denied the basic necessities of life] all over Latin America, there were no other heroes. Che was a necessity, not a possibility; if he hadn't existed, they would have invented him anyway, and often did. The point of the legend was always the same, and as powerful as it was simple: Che lived and died for us.'

Patrick Symmes, from *Chasing Che*.

Timeline

1928	Ernesto Guevara is born in Rosario, Argentina, on 14 May
1930	His first asthma attack
1932	His family moves to Alta Gracia, Argentina
1936–39	Spanish Civil War
1939–45	World War Two
1942–47	Attends high school in Córdoba, Argentina
1948	He enters the University of Buenos Aires to study medicine
1952	January–August: he travels around South America with Alberto Granado
1953	July: he qualifies as a doctor
	August: he leaves on another trip around South America
	December: arrives in Guatemala
1954	Meets Hilda Gadea and Cuban exiles
	June: US-supported invasion of Guatemala
	August: travels in Mexico
1955	July: meets Fidel Castro and agrees to join his revolutionary group
	August: marries Hilda Gadea
1956	February: birth of first daughter Hilda Beatriz Guevara ('Hildita')
	25 November: sets sail with Castro in the *Granma*
	2 December: arrives in Cuba
	5 December: Castro's force almost destroyed in Battle of Alegría de Pío
1957	June: shows great bravery at Battle of El Uvero
	July: promoted to *Comandante*, given command of Second Column
	Autumn: sets up own camp in the mountains
1958	August–October: leads column from Sierra Maestra to the centre of the island
	November: meets Aleida March
	December: Cuban forces win the Battle of Santa Clara
1959	January: arrives in Havana; takes over command of La Cabaña fortress; asks Hilda for divorce; family fly up from Argentina for visit
	January–March: meetings of Tarará group

	May: Agrarian Reform Bill denounced by USA
	June: marries Aleida March
	October: becomes Head of the National Bank
1960	June: US-owned refineries refuse to handle Soviet oil
	July: the US government suspends Cuba's right to sell sugar in USA (it is cancelled permanently in December)
	October: USA imposes trade embargo on Cuba
	November: birth of second daughter Aleida, his first child with Aleida
1961	February: becomes Minister of Industry
	April: the US-supported invasion of Cuba is defeated at Playa Giron (the Bay of Pigs)
1961–63	Cuban economy in steep decline
1962	May: birth of first son, Camilo
	October: Cuban Missile Crisis
1963	June: birth of third daughter, Celia
1963–64	Against his wishes, Cuba forms closer links with the Soviet Union and follows Soviet economic policies
1964	January: Castro agrees long-term economic deal with the Soviet Union
1965	February: Che attacks the Soviet Union in speech in Algiers; birth of second son, Ernesto
	March: returns to Havana from Africa
	April: arrives in Tanzania, and travels to Congo
	May: his mother dies in Argentina
1966	July: last time in Cuba, says goodbye to his children as 'Uncle Ramon'
	November: arrives in Bolivia
	December: meeting with Bolivian communist leader Monje
1967	Feb–March: six-week reconnaissance march
	March: Che's group discovered by Bolivian army
	April: the force is split into two columns
	August: second column ambushed and destroyed
	8 October: first column, under Che, is ambushed. He is captured.
	9 October: murdered by the Bolivian army and buried in a secret location
1997	Che's remains are discovered and flown back to Cuba for re-burial

Key people of Che Guevara's time

Fulgencio Batista (1901–73). The son of a Cuban labourer, Batista rose to power as the leader of an army revolt in 1933, and ruled Cuba as a **dictator** until 1940, when he was elected president. During this first period in power, which ended with an election defeat in 1944, he introduced some much-needed reforms. His second **dictatorship**, which began with another military coup in 1952, was notorious for its corruption and brutality, and he was finally overthrown by Fidel Castro's 26 July Movement early in 1959.

Fidel Castro (1927–). The son of a sugar-planter, Castro studied and practised law in Cuba's capital Havana in the early 1950s. In July 1953 he led an unsuccessful attack on the Moncada barracks in Santiago de Cuba, and was captured and sentenced to fifteen years in prison. Released after two years, he formed the 26 July Movement (named after the date of the attack), and planned and executed a seaborne invasion of Cuba from Mexico. Once established in the mountains of the Sierra Maestra, Castro led a successful civil war against the Batista dictatorship, entering Havana in triumph in January 1959. During the early years of the **revolution**, US hostility towards his policies and aims forced him into a position of dependence on the Soviet Union, which lasted until the collapse of that state in 1991. Despite serious economic difficulties, Castro's regime survived the fall of **communism** in Europe, and he remains a formidable presence, both in Cuba and on the wider world stage.

Laurent Kabila (1938–2001). The leader of the rebels in the area of the Congo chosen by Che for the Cuban support-force. Kabila's unwillingness to assume any direct responsibility for military action was one of the main reasons for Che's frustration in Africa. Thirty years later,

Kabila was the leader of the mixed Congolese-Rwandan forces which overthrew Congo's President Mobutu. However, once in power he showed little interest in improving the conditions of the Congolese people. He was assassinated in 2001 by one of his own bodyguards, for reasons that remain a mystery.

John F. Kennedy (1917–63). Kennedy took office as president of the USA in January 1960. By this time, plans for the invasion of Cuba (the Bay of Pigs) were well under way, and Kennedy, who had insisted that something should be done about Cuba throughout his election campaign, decided to go through with them. When the invasion failed, he ordered a campaign of disruption and **sabotage** ('Operation Mongoose') against the island. On discovering, in the summer of 1962, that there were Soviet missiles in Cuba, he risked a nuclear war to force their withdrawal. He was assassinated in November 1963 (allegedly by a lone assassin called Lee Harvey Oswald).

Nikita Khrushchev (1894–1971). Elected first secretary of the Soviet **Communist** Party in 1953, and over the next few years became the undisputed leader of the Soviet Union. He was in charge during the period of the Cuban Revolution, and presided over Cuba's growing economic and political ties with the Soviet Union, and the Missile Crisis. Failures at home and abroad led to his removal from office by subordinates in 1964.

Places to visit and further reading

Places to visit
The Museum of the Revolution, Havana, Cuba
The Monument of the Train in Santa Clara, Cuba
Moncada Barracks, Santiago, Chile

Websites
www.marxists.org/archive/guevara/

Further reading
The Motorcycle Diaries, Ernesto 'Che' Guevara, Verso, 1995
Fidel Castro: Leader of Cuba's Revolution, Tom Gibb, Wayland, 2000
Heinemann Profiles: Fidel Castro, Sean Connolly, Heinemann Library, 2001

Sources
Che Guevara: A Revolutionary Life, Jon Lee Anderson, Bantam Press, 1999
Compañero: The Life and Death of Che Guevara, Jorge Castañeda, Bloomsbury, 1997
Venceremos! (We Shall Win!) – The Speeches and Writings of Che Guevara, John Gerassi (ed.), Panther, 1968
Back on the Road, Ernesto 'Che' Guevara, Harvill, 2001
Guerrilla Warfare, Ernesto 'Che' Guevara, Pelican, 1969
The African Dream, Ernesto 'Che' Guevara, Harvill, 2001
Bolivian Diary, Ernesto 'Che' Guevara, Cape/Lorrimer, 1968

Glossary

adrenalin naturally-occurring bodily substance which can be used as a stimulant by asthma sufferers

agrarian reform land reform

allergies adverse reactions to certain substances (like particular foods, pollen and dust)

Amazon basin vast area, mostly in Brazil, watered by the River Amazon

amnesty general pardon granted to offenders

Andean Indians indigenous Indians living in the Andes Mountains

asthma disease in which breathing difficulty is caused by excessive contraction of muscles in the tubes connecting the throat with the lungs (see box on page 7)

asylum place of safety. The word is also often used to describe places where the mentally or physically ill have been kept in isolation from the rest of society.

capitalism economic system in which the production and distribution of goods depend on private wealth and profit-making

Cold War name given to the hostility that existed between the capitalist 'West' and communist 'East' between 1947 and the late 1980s

colonial to do with colonies, or the system by which they were ruled (usually refers to the period of European colonialism, between the 15th and 20th centuries)

communism originally an extreme form of socialism, in which property is held communally (in common) rather than individually. The Russian Bolsheviks, who seized power in the second Russian Revolution of 1917, renamed themselves the Russian Communist Party, and the term communism subsequently became associated with the dictatorial state and system of economic planning that was created in the Soviet Union during the 1920s and 1930s.

communist someone who believes in communism

communist bloc communist alliance of states led by the Soviet Union, which included all the East European communist states but Yugoslavia, North Vietnam, North Korea and, until the Chinese-Soviet rift in the early 1960s, China

courier person who carries messages

cremated burned after death

democratically-elected chosen for political office by a free vote of the adult population

developing world poorer parts of the world, which includes most of Africa, Asia and Latin America

dictator person who rules on his/her own, without necessarily taking into account the wishes of the people

dictatorship government by an individual (called a dictator) or a small group that does not allow the mass of the people any say in their government

elite in politics, a small group of people with most political power, most economic power, or a combination of the two

embargo policy of not buying from or selling to a particular nation

exiles people who live outside their own country, whether by choice or not

exploitation taking advantage of, using selfishly or unfairly

guerrilla member of a small armed band, which has usually been formed to fight against either an occupying force or an undemocratic government

guerrilla warfare war fought on one side by unofficial and irregular troops, often in difficult countryside

idealism belief that the world can be made a better place

immigrant someone who comes to settle in another country

imperialism until the mid-20th century, the open political and military domination of weaker states by more powerful ones. Since the mid-20th century, the economic domination of weaker states by more powerful ones.

Inca name of an Indian dynasty which established a large empire around 1200CE in the Andean regions of Peru, Bolivia and Ecuador. It was destroyed by the Spanish in the 1530s.

indigenous native to a particular place, belonging there

land reform changing the pattern of land ownership. Over the last century this has usually meant breaking up large estates owned by wealthy individuals, and handing over the pieces to farmers who have little or no land of their own.

Latin America those areas of the Western Hemisphere which include Spanish-speaking South and Central America, Mexico, the Spanish-speaking Caribbean islands, and Portuguese-speaking Brazil. Some experts argue that French Guiana and the French-speaking Caribbean islands should also be included.

left-wing in politics, usually associated with policies which place the needs of the whole community (everyone) above the short-term wants of the individual. Traditionally, socialism represents a moderate version of this, communism a more extreme one.

leper colony traditionally, an area reserved for those suffering from leprosy, to separate them from the rest of the community

leprosy infectious disease of the skin and nerve-ends (see box on page 16)

mercenaries soldiers fighting in a country other than their own with the sole aim of earning money

mutiny open revolt by lower ranks against superior officers

naval blockade use of ships to prevent other ships reaching a particular destination or country

nobility those who have inherited the membership of the ruling elite

oppression harsh rule

peaceful co-existence name given by the Soviet leaders to their policy of peaceful economic competition with the United States. Once the Soviet Union had proved that communism was economically more successful than capitalism, they argued, then there would no longer be any need for violent revolutions.

peasant farm worker

philosophy study of the causes and nature of human existence

radical far-reaching

rationing system of dividing up an inadequate supply of goods fairly

regime in politics, a government and its supporting organizations

revolution in politics, the overthrow of the existing order in its entirety, not merely the swapping of one group of individuals for another

revolutionary someone committed to supporting and fighting for revolutions

right-wing in politics, usually used to describe people and policies which favour individual interests over those of the community, freedom over equality, and traditional values over radical change

sabotage deliberate damage

security police police force concerned with the security of the state

skirmish brief battle, usually between small groups of soldiers

socialism set of political ideas, which puts more stress on the needs of the community as a whole and less on the short-term wants or needs of the individual

socialist someone who believes in socialism

Spanish Civil War war within Spain (1936–9)

terrorism use of violence against civilian populations – either by states, groups or individuals – with the intention of spreading fear or terror

Index

Alegría del Pío 24
Amazonia 15, 19
Arbenz, President Jacob 19, 20-21, 32
asthma 7

Batista, Fulgencio 23, 24, 25, 26, 28, 29, 30, 31, 37, 58
Bay of Pigs 37, 38, 43, 45, 59
Bella, Ben 47
Bolivia and revolution 4, 18
Buenos Aires 7, 10, 17

capitalism 4, 41, 55
Castro, Fidel 19, 22, 23, 25, 26, 28, 33, 42, 43, 45, 48, 49, 50, 58
Castro, Raul 25
Chile 12, 14
Cienfuegos, Camilo 25, 28
Cold War 5, 36
communism 4, 37, 41, 43, 52-4, 55, 58
Communist Party 6, 32, 44, 49, 50, 59
communists 20, 32, 40, 43, 44, 53
Córdoba 9, 10, 11
Cuba 4-5, 22-4, 31, 36-7
  political reforms in 31-2, 38
  Volunteer Work Programme in 34
Cuban exiles 30, 37
Cuban Missile Crisis 41, 43, 45, 59
Cuban Revolution 4-5, 24, 31, 32, 34, 37, 38, 41, 45, 53, 58, 59

de la Serna y Llosa, Celia (Che's mother) 6, 7, 10, 17, 46-7
dictators 23, 28, 33, 58

Ferrera, Carlos 'Calica' 17, 18, 19

Gadea, Hilda 19, 20, 22, 29, 30, 35
Gandhi, Mahatma 54
Granado, Alberto 11, 14, 16, 19
Granma, the 23, 24, 45
Guatemala 18-20, 22
  US invasion of 20
guerrillas 4, 23, 24-6, 28, 44, 48, 49, 50, 52
Guevara, Ernesto 'Che'
  and the Cuban economy 33-4, 38-9, 53
  and family life 22, 30, 35, 43
  and politics 31, 44, 52
  and socialism 20, 22, 41, 54
  as ambassador for Cuba 32-3, 36
  asthma attacks 7, 9, 10, 15, 20, 27, 31, 46, 51
  birth 6
  'comandante' 26
  death 4-5, 51
  disillusion with the Soviet Union 39-42, 54-5
  education 8, 9, 10
  'El Chancho' 10
  'El Loco' 8
  in Africa 44-7, 53
  in Bolivia 48-51, 53

in Cuba 24-43, 45
in Guatemala 19-21
medical qualifications 17
medical work 25
relationships 10, 12
ruthlessness 25, 27, 30
travels of 11, 12, 14-22
writings of 19, 34, 43

Havana 29, 30, 34-5, 45, 58

Inca civilization 14, 19

Kabila, Laurent 45, 46, 47, 58-9
Kennedy, John F. 42, 59
King Jr., Martin Luther 54
Khrushchev, Nikita 41, 42, 59

La Cabaña fortress 30-31
land reforms 18, 19
'La Poderosa' 12
Latin America 5, 13, 21, 22, 41, 44, 52
Latin-American Indians 13, 14
leper colonies 11, 16, 17
leprosy 16
Lumumba, Patrice 47
Lynch, Ana 6
Lynch, Ernesto Guevara (Che's father) 6

March, Aleida 29, 30, 32, 34-5, 43, 45, 49
Moncada barracks, assault on 19, 22, 23, 58
Monje, Mario 49, 50

Nasser, President 33

rationing 38
Republic of the Congo 44-5, 46, 47
revolutionaries 4, 19, 20, 21, 23, 28, 29, 31, 48

Santa Clara 29, 30
Sierra de Escambray 28
Sierra Maestra 24, 26, 28, 58
Soviet Union 4, 32, 36, 39, 52
  and interests in Cuba 39, 40-43, 45, 50
Spanish Civil War 8-9
Sukarno, President 33

Tshombe, Moise 45
26 July Movement 22, 23, 25, 32, 45, 58

United Fruit 19
USA 4, 32-3, 36, 37
  and Cuba 36, 38, 45
  business interests in Latin America 21

Vallegrande 4-5
Venezuela 12, 16, 19

women's rights 6